Adorably playful illustrations and joyful wordplay will draw in readers of all ages to the beginning of this wonderful collection of nature poems. The first aspect that will capture the reader's attention comes even before the poems begin, when the author writes a little summary of where and why this poetry started, creating the perfect starting-place for us to focus on before diving into the poems themselves. He gives us a small glimpse backwards into a previous age, indicating the powerful influence on certain small childhood moments, which a loving grandmother can bring to bear. The illustrations go well with the whimsical or the more heartfelt poetry-writing. This allows younger children to explore the page with interest as the poems are read aloud. – Airole Warden

CHATTERING AT SCHOOL

(Nature poems for children)

by

Edward Forde Hickey

Grosvenor House
Publishing Limited

The right of Edward Forde Hickey to be identified as the author of this
work has been asserted in accordance with Section 78
of the Copyright, Designs and Patents Act 1988

The book cover is copyright to Jackie Tee

This book is published by
Grosvenor House Publishing Ltd
Link House
140 The Broadway, Tolworth, Surrey, KT6 7HT.
www.grosvenorhousepublishing.co.uk

This book is a work of fiction. Any resemblance to
people or events, past or present, is purely coincidental.

A CIP record for this book
is available from the British Library

ISBN 978-1-80381-192-5

CHATTERING AT SCHOOL
(Nature poems for children)

by

Edward Forde Hickey

Grosvenor House
Publishing Limited

The right of Edward Forde Hickey to be identified as the author of this
work has been asserted in accordance with Section 78
of the Copyright, Designs and Patents Act 1988

The book cover is copyright to Jackie Tee

This book is published by
Grosvenor House Publishing Ltd
Link House
140 The Broadway, Tolworth, Surrey, KT6 7HT.
www.grosvenorhousepublishing.co.uk

This book is a work of fiction. Any resemblance to
people or events, past or present, is purely coincidental.

A CIP record for this book
is available from the British Library

ISBN 978-1-80381-192-5

This book is
dedicated to Grannie and Jack

Back in the years 1951/58 - during my school holidays at grannie's little farm in Dolla (Tipperary) - I found enough peace and quiet to scribble a few hurried drafts for the following verses before heading back to my parents and the smoky landscape of London. Each day grannie and her son, Jack, would go off to the cowshed to milk their cows. But before that - and to encourage me - she would give me a pencil and a post-office copybook so that I could try my hand at writing - something she knew I liked to do. As a result, I often found myself behind the hay-reek (on sunny days) or above in the old hayshed (on rainy days) with nothing but the wind in the trees to disturb me as I wrote down my thoughts.

From the age of 11 up until I was 18 - as soon as I made my sad journey from Tipperary back to school in West Kensington - I tailored these schoolboy efforts as best I could and sent my humble collection back to grannie to read during the cold winter nights. These unadorned pieces have remained private and hidden for the past 64 years. But now, in my old age – and looking at them with fresh eyes - I feel that they might bring a bit of pleasure to one or two younger readers - my own grandchildren among them - and encourage them to write.

Edward Forde Hickey. May 2022

Contents

Contents

GREEDY CROCODILE

Weary old me on
the sandy bank,
I'm always getting
thinner.
Time I crocodiled my way
To the river for my dinner.

Plump fat me in the afternoon bush,
ready for my tea.
Time I crocodiled in again
For fish and sympathy

Full to the brim in the twilight glow,
washed and scrubbed for bed.
Time I crocodiled to sleep,
contented lad, well fed.

Bless me, what about tomorrow?
I must hunt once more.
Think I'll crocodile a different
tastier stretch of shore.

PENGUIN

I'm only a silly old penguin.
I'm almost two years old.
My feet are meant for dancing with.
That's what I've been told.

I'm only a silly old penguin,
painted black and white.
My colours are such that I can be seen
at any hour of the night.

I have thousands of relations,
who huddle close to me.
I don't mind being a penguin
at the edge of the Polar Sea.

Everyone to his own taste.
Kindly let me be:
a cheerful, clumsy
slip-of-a penguin - that,
my friends, is me!

OSTRICH

Does he – no, I don't believe it –
hide his head in sand?
Better ostrich pastimes surely
were ordained and planned.

For you have legs to race with
at energetic speed.
And my advice – the use of them –
that is all you need.

Get yourself away from here
over the bushland wild.
The grass beyond the mountaintops
is juicier, more mild.

See far-distant places,
utilise your mind.
Get a move on, ostrich,
sand can make you blind.

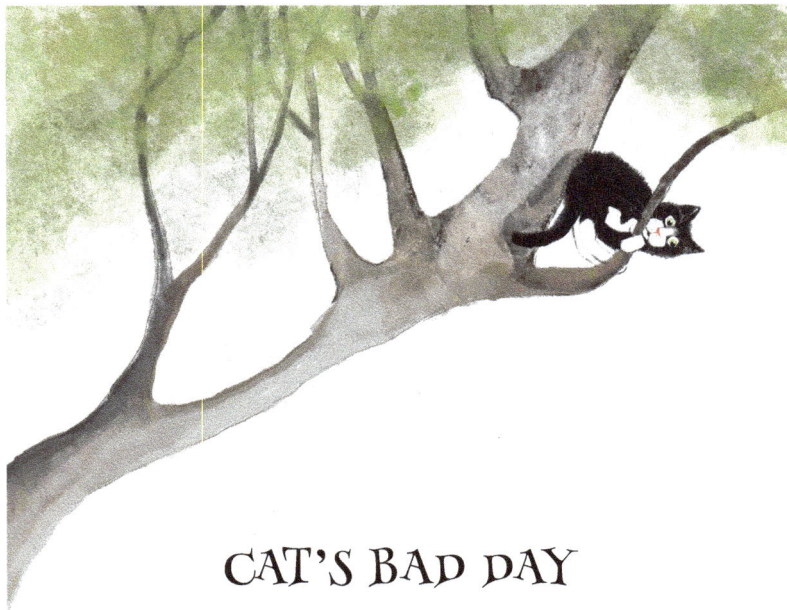

CAT'S BAD DAY

I was crossing over Old Joe's alley,
when - suddenly – alarm!
Old Joe's big Brutus made a dash,
his teeth unveiled for harm.

Oh, I dashed, I dashed in a headlong
tizzy down to Gretta's shack.
I could hear each snarl, I could feel
the fur rising on Brutus's back.

But what to do?
No time for panic.
Find me the nearest tree.
A lung-tearing leap - heart-thumping -
then at last I reach safety.

Upwards, upwards now I circle.
(Steady as you go).
I've reached the top but now I'm scared
as I gaze at the fields below.

The hay-barns spinning, lanes whiz-
whizzing, children stop and stare.
ring-a-ding, ting-a-ling – fireman's bell.
Danger! Where? Up there!

A sweating fireman, panting, cursing,
anger in each sigh.
Up on the ladder, heavenwards lumbering,
craning his thunderous eye.

Meeow! Please fireman, don't be angry!
Brutus is the knave.
Gretta's shack and Old Joe's alley
were nearly Suzie's grave!

CHEETAH

The speed, sheer windy
speed that flashes by,
as the cheetah urges on his lengthy span.
An ill-fated gazelle, fast, yet not fast enough…
Catch me if you can.

I can.

A zebra, twin-barred, mesmerizing colours,
has drawn the cheetah speeding down the hill.
An urgent answer in his thunderous shape.
Catch me if you will.

I will.

The ambling antelope, as he picks sweet grasses
seemingly unhurried, homeward bending.
The cheetah, speed of lightning, quickly flashes.
Catch me if…

you know the sudden ending.

Have you not seen a cheetah in a book –
imagined - and then marveled at his flight?
A flash before his gradual extinction,
a speed unparalleled, a wondrous sight.

I know you have.

LION-KILL

A herd of deer
the lion sees.
The reindeer suddenly
quake at the knees.

The lion dashes
in to seize
a reindeer.
They all seem to freeze.

Utmost panic.
Hearts that quake.
One lunge, the lion
a deer's life will take.

Fate, pure fate
of the weaker kind,
who never troubled
to look behind.

CATERPILLARS

Sunning themselves in the afternoon heat,
free for a while to roam,
lazily plodding from leaf to leaf,
blind in their garden home.

So many friends in the afternoon heat,
not a leaf left for Jack's pet rabbits.
Grannie comes along day in and day out
to conclude their feeding habits.

Big white butterflies dance on the cabbage.
I've seen as many as ten.
Grannie in a rage waltzes out with her spray.
When she's gone, they'll be back again.

Whilst sunning themselves in the afternoon heat,
free for a while to roam.
fruits for the blackbirds,
fat green caterpillars,
extend their garden home.

Grannie, if you want any peace at all,
there's but one means of redress:
get Jack to stop sowing rows of cabbage
till the caterpillars change their address.

THE OWL

In old grannie's hedgerow Owl
sits high in the tree,
With the harvest moon his halo, he
peers down at you and me.
Not a sound does he make,
though to rouse him our
catapults take delight,
The day's his time for sleeping,
he's tired from carousing all night.
Solemnly hooting at mid-night,
world of the fox and the bat,
soaring into the quiet moonlight -
in God's holy name, what's that?
Downy-winged is his journey.
Homewards you and I saw
Owl with a sad-looking fieldmouse
firmly stuck in his claw.
What an eye he's got, our swift hunter,
how wise he can contemplate,
as the vole in old grannie's hedgerow
runs for his life - too late!
A hoot for his wisdom, I tell you,
I cannot help underrating,
for the little wren rides on his back
when this wise old owl is migrating!

CROWFOXED

Caw, said the crow to the cunning old fox,
dropping the cheese from its mouth.
Mother and father, brothers and sisters,
all of them are gone out.

Gone to the field beyond Corcoran's Well,
and the corn uncle Jack has sowed.
Only I am at home, very sick with a cold,
in Sam's lofty rookery abode.

They'll be back, never fear, in the twilight dusk
when the cows amble up Hickey's lane.
They'll be back in the rookery, heady and healthy,
full to their bellies with pain.

What tales will be told in the evening nests
of Billy Boy's scarecrow and gun.
What plans for Pat Collin's garnering tomorrow
after day's feasting is done.

But now I'm stuck here, said the crow to the fox.
You see I'm too frail to go out.
But the fox had long gone
with the fine lump of cheese
that had dropped from
the sick crow's mouth.

CRICKETS A-PLENTY

I saw

old Grannie with her candle cross the floor.
She killed the thirtieth cricket at the half-door.
The turf perhaps, or maybe 'twas the rain,
had brought them in again.

I was

sleeping in the Tall Room, snug in bed,
long time after the thirtieth cricket lay dead,
when from the depths of the finished ashen fire
I suddenly heard a choir.

I heard

chirps re-echoing through the ghostly house,
frightening in the rafters rat and mouse.
Grannie from her bedroom gave a peep
and then went back to sleep.

CALF OF SIX HOURS

Liver-nosed bundle of white and of chestnut,
could I but grow back, become new like you,
could I but share in your little anxieties,
look upon life with the blur of your vision,

perhaps, it is then – it is then, only then –
that I'd have for myself the meaning of life,
become innocent, fragile as you are now,
as stainless as your pair of morning eyes.

A stone-throw away from your struggle for milk,
lies the sunshiny gleam of Bridgie's red flowers,
the birds' merry nuptials atop Mikey's trees
and the cats somersaulting inside Timmy's shed.

They're mere scraps of-paper on this summer's day
in your presence, your glory, your wonderous aplomb,
mere shady hobgoblins, as though fast asleep,
when compared to your spirited, beautiful face.

POOR ASS, NED

Poor cantankerous Ned!

Unsure and bewildered though your eyes are now,
yet from their sadness a message comes clear
as a sunbeam, fresh from your lonely sick bed
on the cold, ghostly straw inside Tim Meara's shed
where death's grasping fingers are cruelly lurking,
awaiting your bronchial limbs' final sigh.

No more you'll revive your famed legs of the past,
that once kicked asunder the old fellow's cart,
for your heart's pulse has fizzled away to a thread.
Accept now your fate – for, like us, you must-
in the pit that Tim Meara's sad spade has just dug,
to the left of the beckoning whitethorn tree.

Poor beleaguered Ned!

ROE-BUCKS WERE FIGHTING

I witnessed two huge antlered stags
fighting on our Bull-Paddock green,
down in our valley so shady
where the sun refused to be seen.

Their prize, she sat contentedly,
watching this dreadful fray.
A shame to think that one of them
would have to slink away!

No need to sing the contest
or which of them had won.
A shame, a cruel and worthless shame
that it ever was begun.

BAT

A bat, with no friends to call his own,
    slept the livelong day.
When dusk came on, he shook himself.
    To his work he flew away.

He crossed Jack Rohan's sleeping corn
    and dipped among the briar.
He scanned the hedgerows everywhere,
    his supper to acquire.

Hawk-like, always on the prowl,
    creature velvet and fat,
your mother trained you well
    to hunt,
villainous web-winged bat.

DEERSHOCK

He comes from Mucklin's hillslope
down to the water's edge.
He sees his morning reflection
as he looks down o'er the ledge.

Senseless laughter above him
is suddenly overheard
and, looking up, his eyes behold
an early mocking jaybird.

Leaving the Dolla's sunlit stream
with its daylight glacier chill,
the young deer ambles out the gap
and up towards Mountisland hill.

Neath glossy leaves he carelessly strays
'midst Jack Scissors' thistles and dock,
fresh in woodland knowledge,
fragile-limbed his stock.

And later on, strange thoughts are his
as he looks at a twinkling star -
to think how truly beautiful
                    his river reflections are!

LADYBIRDS

There's a ladybird in my soup, Grannie.
Grannie, I *am* being serious.
Took a wrong turn from the rest of the fold,
a phenomenon most mysterious.

This summer there's ladybirds everywhere.
When did they all arrive?
It can't be – it is! – I've seen twenty-four.
Now how do they all survive?

Little yellow eggs on the leaf on the tree,
little yellow eggs on the thorn,
little yellow eggs no more to be seen,
all hatched in the heat of the morn.

There's a ladybird saved from my soup, Grannie,
on a hanky laid out cold.

Back to his horde he'll be carried once more
like a prodigal son to the fold.

On a leaf I place my soup-stained ladybird.
Thankless six-legs, you're free.
Child of the wild-world, gone to his brothers,
saved by a child's sympathy.

It can't be right to see so many
with black dots one to seven.
This summer there's ladybirds everywhere.
Must be a ladybird's heaven.

Little yellow eggs on the leaf on the tree,
little yellow eggs on the thorn,
little yellow eggs no more to be seen,
all hatched in the heat of the morn.

There's a greenfly in my soup, Grannie.
Oh, you never think I'm serious.
"I suppose he took a wrong turning too!"
Now this is more than mysterious.

FISHES IN THE OCEAN

I want to go to sea one day to the sailors' watery home.
I want to enter secret caves beneath the swishing foam
where mermaids dance a sea-blue ballet,
gliding through the deep,
where music weaves a spell that lulls the dreamy fish to sleep.
And maybe – surely - there will be a galleon to explore,
old chests with maps and shiny treasure,
swords and guns galore.
What mysteries to puzzle on, what new imaginary scene,
waiting for me to venture in where no-one else has been.
I'll bring back sea anemones, orchids, pearls new,
and I shall bring back patterned shells and
stones of brilliant hue.
But all the fishes of the ocean I shall leave to roam
and swim to their eternal rest beneath the swishy foam.

KILLER-WHALE

Who wouldn't be a killer,
when faced with the eye of Man
and yet wouldn't turn and swim away
with a 'catch-me-if-you-can?'

The whale in that dark immensity
fears the threat of the boat.
Yet, hope of the whole of his family,
his spirit keeps him afloat.

This whale a killer now will be
as he dashes forth to attack.
He challenges so ferociously
that the sailors are taken aback.

Fearfully they rush about.
It's terrible to behold.
Sheer terror in each pitiful shout,
bloodied waters, so we're told!

KITTEN-CAT

This kitten, like a fluffy dandelion,
his tail a curling angry whip behind,
is chasing insects, birds and butterflies,
his playful fur blowing in the wind.

Lady Dunally in her garden green,
sunhat, sunglasses, suntan cream,
fruit, a knitting basket, magazines
and wool unravelling - a kitten's dream!

Round one, draw out the frightened head of wool,
and strike it with your talons till afraid.
Submission. Now lead out your bidden slave.
Triumphant, through the bright flowerbeds parade.

Round two, the dance. How clever! What an art!
To right and left and up the centre too.
turning, twisting, interweaving moves,
but now the wool, encaptured, captures *you*!

A web? A prison? Sheer entanglement
Oh, clever kitten, and such enterprise!
Your once-proud freedom cul-de-sacced at last,
and a laughing mistress, feigning her surprise.

Your playful anger and your strength to kill
have all been mangled at the earliest sweep.
But she'll unloose your tiny frame and then
in arms warm you can purr yourself to sleep.

THE MOUSE, THE RAT AND THE CAT

In Jack's cornfield
was a mouse and he
lived very well.
Hayseeds for breakfast,
dinner and tea,
If the truth of an honesty
I must tell.

In his farmyard was a rat.
He too lived very well.
He had hayseeds, turnips, spearmint and docks,
If the truth of an honesty I must tell.

In the house there was a cat
and he lived very well.
He had mice and rats, and rats and mice
If the truth of an honesty I must tell

So, the mouse had hayseeds all day
and the rat lived on turnip stew
But the cat took the insects and turnips,
rats and mice for his Sunday brew.

Do I care for the cat, you ask me,
well-fed with a mouse and a rat?
Rascal of rascals, I could skin him alive,
demonical well-fed cat!

Take the house and the farmyard too,
add the cornfield, all in a row.
Share the profits with mouse, rat, cat,
and ask me the answer, I'll write it below:

"Live all ye creatures, great and small
and grant life to others, one and all."

POLAR BEAR

I sit upon the ice
and I gaze upon a dark revolving cloud.
Here, high up in the north,
to live just as I please I am allowed.

No fish, no animal
escapes my hunting, everyone is snatched.
The colour of my coat
by lumps of foamy iceberg flakes is matched.

I sit on the frozen stuff
and on me falls a sprinkling heap of snow.
The seal beneath the ice
is nurturing himself for me, I know.

PIGEON DANCE

Pigeons, bright as snow above
the busy market-day street,
arc and arch, loom, then dive,
to land on dizzy feet.

Gliding in upon their runway
where no eye can see.
Busy birds for love's fiesta,
in their solitarie.

Silence. Oh, their loving meeting,
flowing joy entwined.
Searching hearts and beating rhythm,
aloof from our mind.

Coo, Coo! They strut there, dreamily
upon the parapet's edges.
Sheer delight, this busy Spring,
for two young pigeons' pledges.

PUPPY FOR GRANNIE

Six little puppies out in the barn, once on a
snow-covered morn,
as the wild gale howled
on roofs and shutters,
to Fran their mother were born.

Milk and a kindly growl from Fran as she gazed
at each one-day-old,
snug in the manger with
sacks and straw and a coat to keep out the cold.

One day - another – and then a week,
unsteady, they waddled about
from the bike to the barrow and back again,
each step a riotous rout.

They were given some milk in an old tuna tin
and bread mashed up in a
tray.
They spilt the milk and
they tumbled
the buckets that awaited
the calves
each day.

But the joy of an early
childhood
only lasts for a fleeting week.
For Grannie came out with a wave of her stick
and she pointed at me, Pip-Squeak.

Silky-eared, wet-nosed, trouble
and fun,
I was taken from mother that
day,
a present to comfort Gran's
lonesome fireside
since Grandad had passed away.

But still there is Tom, Sara, Jack,
Bill, Peg.
They'll roam for another week.
And then, who knows? They
may come and stay
with grannie and me,
Pip-Squeak.

And what of Fran, my mother so proud,
who cared for us, might and main?
She'll be sad and lonely for
a month and a day.
Then, she'll start all over again.

DONKEY MISERY

At the best of times there's a cross upon my back,
a saddle and tackling, a creamery cart behind.
Rain seeps through where I sleep in Morrisey's shack.
My master, a heedless wretch, has never been kind.

With briars the children thump me under the tail
to see me kick my hind legs in the air
or they fetch a branch to beat me from the dyke.
Heedless children, as if I didn't care.

If you had logs to fetch from Clonmore Wood
and wretched flies to bleed your eyes each day,
children to scorn and torment your harmless flesh,
perhaps you too would have something sad to say.

They ride on my back, I pitch them from on high.
They renew their cursing efforts peevishly.
A crestfallen heap they lie low in the nettles.
As time and again I deny them furiously.

I wish I could leave this hateful Curryquinn..
I wish I could travel down to the edge of the sea.
For one or two carrots of homage I'd carry the whole
load of children from dawn right up until soda bread tea.

FROGGY FROG

Grannie trudges over the meadow grass,
Nearby sits Uncle Jack on his moving-car green.
Music and magic, the hay soon falling dead,
'near the smoky blue of a sky, for a while serene.

Meanwhile, in the rushy, undrained acres
Froggy in hasty childhood greets the day,
hopping nearer to the danger zone
where Jack's machine is treacherously on its way.

The purr of the engine, cry of the husband-man,
speed of the oncoming, well-oiled mowing-car blade.
ah, the instant tattered remains of a headstrong youth,
and the waiting heart-stricken kin in the evening shade.

In the night frogs sadly croak beside our pool
They echo a mystified dirge for their murdered son.
Unadventurously we live and we know it's best:
not too little or much - just enough to have done.

I listen to frogs croaking near our pool.
A mating croak, a mourning croak? Advice?
I feel on the painful death of Froggy Frog
the message addressed is simple:

FROGS THINK TWICE.

DOG OF ALL TRADES

As a puppy he was always good,
as a young dog better still.
And I daresay he was 'middle-o'-the-road'
in the days he was 'over the hill'.

He could beg, he could roll over,
and he strictly obeyed my laws.
He could 'speak up' or show submission,
with his head tucked between his paws.

If I held a stick out yonder,
he would leap it at my commands.
From the ditch at a "here boy!" call from me
he would bound right into my hands.

When the cows were needed I'd only to say
"Go fetch them, my loyal and true".
Obedient, joyful, away he would scurry,
to lead them with no more ado.

The fox, who lived near our Bull-Paddock field,
a stranger (he'd too much senses!)
apprehensively hid in the heart of Bog Wood,
with his young ones behind the barbed fence.

Not another dog in our valley
had a wish but to be the friend
of Rover, whose virtues were all superb.
Ah, well – that's all come to an end.

For he died – it was early last springtime,
when the young fields were crisp and green,
that I honoured his grave with a bucket of my tears -
the best dog that I'd ever seen.

PIGEON-FACE

Down from the tree Missy
Wagtail flew,
joyously, wings outspread.
I'd know Missy Wagtail any day or night,
she's a streak of white on her head.

With a flap of her tail and a dawn salute
she sits on the sun-drenched lawn.
My crumbs cut small for breakfast she tackles,
then back to her tree she's gone.

She's pleased with the way that her bright morning sings,
but soon a surprise lies ahead.
With an old-fashioned waddle enters the scene
Pigeon-face, still to be fed.

Oh, the greedy old fellow, what a stomach to fill
as he breaks through the morning flowers.
Poor wee wagtail, shamelessly cast out,
having waited since the early hours.

Days went by - oh, if I had a gun! –
I forgot old Pigeon-face,
till one day Puss made a mess of his tail
and he vanished without a trace.

Bless me, listen to the rest of the tale.
I was sitting in Market Square,
reading my Dickens and waiting for Sean,
no plans, not a single care.

I was munching a sandwich of pickles and cheese
when a misty form I could trace.
There on the bench and begging for a crumb -
well I never! – old Pigeon-face.

His tail in tatters, lonely and forlorn,
of his once-proud bearing not a trace.
Well, I gave him the last of my pickles and cheese.
All's forgiven, old Pigeon-face.

I know what Missy Wagtail would surely twitter
if she knew that we two were here.
For I often meet Pigeon-face while I'm waiting
for Sean here in Market Square.

GOLDFISH

Goldfish bowl in a sunny window,
a prison, protecting the blind.
Heated glass, unnatural diet,
but a goldfish has no mind.

You've acres of water to swim in, Fishy,
Mind your tail as you turn.
Surely a goldfish bowl is nothing
more than a funeral urn.

HEDGEHOG

One night as I was strolling along,
a form I happened to spy.
Was it a cat or was it a rat?
No – a hedgehog very close by.

I kept him in my view, of course,
not that the hedgehog cared.
He couldn't see where he was walking,
for danger unprepared.

A cruel man it must have been,
who had placed upon its nose
an ice-cream cone with sticky boiled sweets –
a mirthful joke, I suppose.

This way - that way - down Timmy's lane
the poor old hedgehog scurried.
I left my friends at the end of the gap
and after him I hurried.

Catching the cone, I gave it a tug.
not a sound from the poor hedgehog.
Freed at last. Then I ran home to bed
where I slept as sound as a log.

Next day I chanced to be passing again
the hedgehog's regular beat
and there in the lane, the hedgehog – dead.
He had failed to make his retreat.

THE ROBIN, THE EEL
AND THE DEER

In a ferny glade lives an eel
and a robin, his life-long friend.
In Clonmore Wood live a dozen deer,
browsing, time without end.

Hugging this spot from the winds all around
are the Mucklin slopes supreme.
Evening peace, interrupted by cows
coming down to drink at Phil's stream.

Man himself has never been known
to enter this haven of peace.
The eel and the robin, the untroubled deer
without him they daily increase.

Keep to your cabins, keep to your farms,
sit by your warm turf-fire
and leave them this peace in their ferny glade,
the joys of the wild to admire.

FOX AND LAMB

Wintertime and a fox on the prowl,
bends his way to the fold.
Wintertime and a lamb just born
on the hillside, shivering, cold.
See the fox's inevitable track
to the haven he knows best.
See the lamb, so snug and warm
in the wool of his mother's vest.
"I hear," says the fox, "that a lamb is born.
What a tender morsel for me!
So, I must waylay the sheep this night,
since hunger and I disagree."
Enter the field and circle the fold.
"Do you see the lamb so mild?
Now tell me, fox, have you
the heart to hurt a new-born child?
Haven't you young ones
yourself at home
the cold night to
endure?
And their mother
dotes on them just the
same with milk and
comfort sure."
It's true," said the fox,
"you've struck a blow
for the innocent and the meek.
I'll wend my way to Clonmore Wood,
more worthy gains to seek."

SEAGULLS

Watchful seagulls, silently on high,
diligently guide our good ship home.
A steady faithful compliment they seem
masters, ever skilful, of the foam.

We view them sitting on the gunwale rest.
They curl away like windblown kites and dip
for proffered titbits, biscuits, buns and crisps,
thrown by city children down from the ship.

Harmlessly these birds of discipline swoop,
ever watchful, always hoping something fresh to gain,
when a spiteful youth, without a care in the world,
throws a burning cigarette out into the main.

Dots, amid the white seahorses, bobbing
with skilful antics in the musical foam,
drawing always our youthful attention
as they sway, forever buoyantly at home.

Their sentinel, their leader, watch-cries giving,
espies each stirring from his perched flag-pole.
Fearlessly, this long accustomed day-tripper
watches his inferiors' showy parole.

And as they reach out, nearer to the shore,
their brethren fly out from the Emerald Isle,
joining them in their merry swooping antics,
vying in grandeur with them for a while.

And just before our good ship sights the land,
harbour-ward the beckoning seagulls fly.
And when our ship is anchored to the quay,
they offer a welcome from their perch on high.

In spite of our attention, they must journey soon
and on the beach play out their afternoon.
And then they will retreat to Wicklow's heights,
to nests intangible for love's delights

THE RUNAWAY HORSE

We were dancing with the treetops,
we were prancing in a storm
when the viciousness of Man appeared
and tried to shape a form
that would suit his way of travel,
that would change us from our own.
To be set on by such evils -
to a horse, a thing unknown.

Well, we rallied and we smarted,
but it wasn't worth our while.
for the viciousness of Man, it seems.
was brother to his guile.
And a reins from nowhere curling
drew the life-breath from my frame.
I was snatched away from Nature
and from parents, both the same.

To Ned's Forge and to a training place
for the fray in time led forth.
Inside a ring of moon-faced men
lay my value and my worth.
Ah, shame! I pined away and staggered
underneath the tongue
and the viciousness of Man, poor fools,
to think I'd bear it long.

When early dawn squashed out her redness
through each cart-wheel's spoke,
I strained my every sinew
and from bitter shackles broke.
Mick-the-Herd's ferns and grasses
then stringed their welcoming strain
as hooves of freeborn flint went twinkling
unoppressed again!

THE NIGHTINGALE

The blackcap, the chaffinch, the blackbird and thrush,
all enter the contest, but I'm in no rush.

Day in and day out, they sing songs while it's light.
Then I sing my song at the death of twilight.

The throstle's melodious, or so I have heard.
And it's said I'm no sweeter than many a bird.

Yet all of these songsters are hushed in mute rage
when I for my aria take to the stage.

The sweetest of music in unsullied note,
night in and night out I pour from my throat.

Though my rivals sing songs when it's dawn's early light,
I've the woods for myself in the dark of the night.

DEER-DEATH

Lads were working hard in the burning noon,
Chopping tall timbers, 'twould be lunchtime soon.
More foresters were weeding out and planting,
when nearer they were brought to a young deer panting.

'twas well-gone after tea when the news I heard.
They had caught the deer, a-quivering like a bird.
They held a billhook and sickle over its head.
Tim ended their dire devilry and the deer away he led.

Setting it free, only to damage again
new saplings on the far side of the drain.
Hearing Tim's wild curses, in alarm
the deer leapt into the drain - irreparable harm.

Look at him, broken-necked - pity him lying there.
Foresters, scorn him now, if one of you dare:
a cast-off wonder, noble son of the wild,
Beauteous deer, Nature's brief-lived child.

BUDGIE ERROR

A budgie perch in a budgie cage,
deserted now, a sad outrage.

For budgie's cage-door opened wide
and he took a trip to the other side.

A budgie's swing and a budgie's mirror,
useless now through a budgie error

Budgie bath and budgie seed,
what's the point? No bird to feed.

Cage for a budgie's a prison wall.
Yet it's better than having no home at all.

A cat, content in the sunny weather,
licks from his jaws the last sad feather.

NEW-DAY ANIMALS

This night, heavy with stars, departs our croft.
In the smoky eye of morn there rear aloft
warbling birds, their feathers poppy soft.

It is the grey of dawn.

Foxes new-born, yelp whilst the sun is outpoured
and recent pregnant mares come drink at the ford.
Rabbits sip the dew, their cold eyes lowered.

It is the grey of dawn.

The reindeer squabble close to Dunally's lake.
In the furze the double-bleak of the corncrake.
Aimlessly young flies through the clearing break.

It is the grey of dawn.

Behind our gander, innocent, not for long,
Tim's wildcat, hid in the bushes, stalks along.
The moon's bright gleam cast out by blackbird's song.

It is the grey of dawn.

THE COCK THAT DIDN'T CROW

The cockerel didn't bother to crow.
It was dark when Matty Symons drove down
a fine collection of thirty-seven cattle,
his and his neighbours'.

He left them all through the night
In Old Pat Collin's lower Pool Field,
ready for the dawn drive into Nenagh.
It was dark when he stopped at Kindy's Drinking-House,
his lips very dry for whiskey,
warming his cockles for the long drive in.

Dark too when grannie Forde,
that jewel of mine, in this heartless morning
poured out the strength and warmth of her smiling
across the table and the feather-shelled egg.
With her toothless smiles she tried to undermine
my wish to return to the blankets and sleep's nest.

Still dawn when she buffeted me out of my gloom.
"See the pretty flowers all over the hawthorn bush,
white as the snow, and the pink of the fuchsias,
and shivering honeysuckle on the pig-house bush,
languourly drinking in its dewy rain-food,
and the turbulent wind combing out the grass
along the haggart ditch."

Meanwhile, scholars tramp the well-trodden path
down Mountisland slope. Brave children,
turning their jaw from the wind and the rain.
A misty bike, its headlamp burning,
comes crashing through the drizzle, passed our stream.

I follow Jack from the half-door to the yard.
Part of me - the kiss of my grannie on my cheek-
remains behind me with my aged guardian.
A single moment - a heart that touches a heart -
and she to the left of the morning - I to the right.
Monday morning and the cock hadn't crowed - till then.

COCKEREL SIREN

On our dung-heap, our stinking old dung-heap,
black, green and purple with age
there sentinelled a proud cockerel,
showing off his bright plumage.

And on many another dung-heap,
covered with sour-smelling grass,
sat many more colourful cockerels,
waiting for time to pass.

Our geese and their young in the hen-house
lay dreaming of meadows rare,
and the soft yellow chicks in a tea-chest bed
were asleep, not a solitary care.

The fox had avoided their roost that morn
as he swam through the acres of dew.
Only owls and bats and a wildcat's wail
and our watch dog, loyal and true.

Then a trumpet, a clarion, loud and shrill,
re-echoed from mountain and vale.
One cockerel, two - then a hundred more –
over Nature to crow and prevail.

You may talk of the train's loud whistle
or the note of the factory bell.
You have never been near to the classical strains

of a rum-bust-i-ous
cockerelle!

SNAKE

5 4

Why are you hiding high above me
'midst the tropical trees?
Why are you groveling far below me?
Snake, communicate – please!

"I am alone, like my brother the worm,
a cast-out history says,
all for the sake of the firstborn snake,
who sadly fell from God's grace.

On our bellies we slide and we slink away,
to hide in some rocky cave.
We are covered by earth, covered by shame,
our recompense made in our grave."

Never mind, poor Snaky, spare your poison,
others save from harm.
Your turn, full circle, will one day come,
to endow the world with your charm.

So, come down from your hiding-place above,
feel the touch of an amorous breeze.
Leave venom behind you, dance with the world,
relax with us, take your ease.

No more hiding high above me
'mongst the tropical trees.
No more groveling far below me.
Snake – communicate- please!

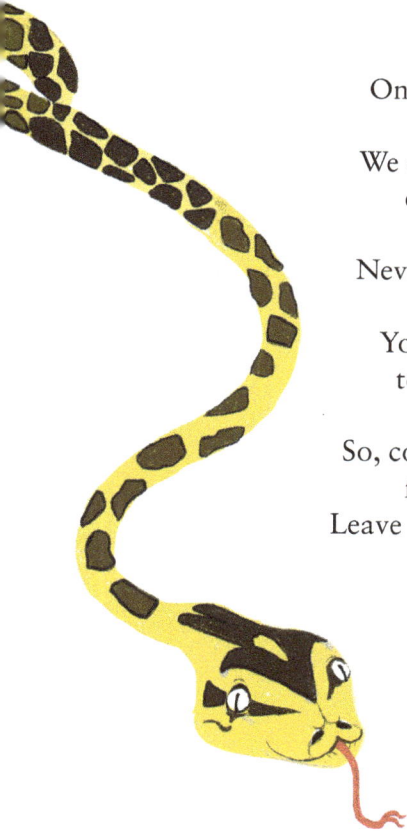

FOXY REDMAN

Do you – no, of course you
don't –
see what I can see,
as I sit a magpie mother
high in Minogue's oak tree?
Gently lapping like the water
In the stream below,
Foxy Redman, lightly
tripping
on his delicate toe.

Thank whoever I must thank
my babies four now sleep
and mother lies in wonderland
after her long days reap.
Hedges edging, sly fox moving,
gates and fences passed.
Grasses, dew-flowers, through them shoving,
to the farmer's yard at last!

56

Loud his heart is beating, swiftly
at the gate he sways.
He barks uncertain in the moonlight,
far away his gaze.
No answering echo from the watchdog.
What good chance for gain!
First the dung-heap, then the henhouse.
"Soon I'll be home again."

Easy, stealthily - instant kill,
my young ones I must reach."
Then an aching chasm - a volleying shot –
A fox in Death's long breech.
Uncertain timing? Too unwary?
Now his cunning crown
from Foxy Redman by my uncle's
fusillade has been blown.

ZEBRA-TALK

Brother and kin to the whole of the wild,
I was scarcely born, when a motherless child.

If you had to save your generation,
you'd quickly learn about preservation.

I wish some man would capture me,
on a reservation make me unfree.

Without the fear of the unknown wild,
I would settle down, though a motherless child.

Brother and kin to the horse, that's me.
There's just one difference, I am free.

Free, for my fretted blood to be spilled.
Free, to be mauled and brutally killed.

DADDY-LONG-LEGS

Please stop grumbling, Long-legs!

I'm tired of crashing into cowshed walls
with all these legs of mine, so very weak and frail,
I'm tired of dragging eight legs all my life.
What on earth, I ask you, does it avail?

Oh, do be quiet, Long-legs!

Yesterday one damaged, a terrible loss.
Today another wrenched, a dreadful plight.
Tomorrow, maybe another long one broken.
Always and ever fright upon fright upon fright.

For heaven's sake, be quiet, Long-legs!

You must, my dear – you absolutely must
(other Long-legs put up with life the same)
take more precautions where you find you're walking
and realize how spindly is your frame.

Keep on listening, Long-legs.

Think about your brothers, who are dead,
held by the sticky death-trap, dreadful blight!
Better to be injured than be taken
by the gummed flypaper underneath the light!

So, for heaven's sake, stop grumbling, Long-legs!

BOY'S DAYDREAM

Mountisland, well-watered, fertile, rare,
where a boy sat down 'neath an old oak tree,
that grew in grandeur in that pleasant sphere,
attacked not by fog nor the wind's enmity.
At noonday he lay, surrounded by peace,
the grass crisp as fern-stems in every place.
close to Tim's meadow, adorned with new poppies,
blissfully captured in Nature's embrace.
He dozed and he dreamed of harvest-time mowing,
of thirsty, tired workers saving their corn,
of haybarns hereafter full to overflowing,
of a thrashing-machine, soon silent and forlorn.

Later at twilight beneath the high trees
that o'erhang John's Gate not far from the stream,
he listened awhile to the minstrelsies
of Mikey's fat pigeons on fir-trees' high beam.
Their dry, throaty warbling had gladdened his heart
with reveries of summer, too soon to depart.
And over the farm in the hills all around
he could hear re-echoing the giddy sound
of Tommy Sir's sheep hastening home to the pen,
their day's roaming done till the sun rose again.
And there he remained till the blackbirds' last cries
hushed to sleep all the hills with their lullabies.

ADVICE FROM NATURE

When you have worked your fingers to the bone
for food and shelter and a place to dwell
and when you have obtained these simple joys,
by then it's time to bid the world farewell.

Patterns for your living take from Nature
and struggle not too much nor yet too small.
For just enough is all you need for living
and more than that is nothing gained at all!

Author's Note

A *year or two prior to those blissful summer holidays in Dolla, I had written a verse or two (idle chattering), while sitting on my own after coming home from school. Then burglars came and stole some of our family possessions from our basement flat in West London - among them, my little collection of stamps and my numerous attempts to write a few lines. These youthful efforts had been typed out by my teacher and given back to me in a neat little black folder, of which I was very proud. I could not understand the robbers' cruelty. 'What on earth are these robbers going to do with my child's poems - make paper planes out of them?' said my mother ruefully.*

I remember my first short verse, written one sunny Saturday morning as I lay in the long grass near the tennis court inside Queen's Park Recreation Ground in Paddington, and which I posted back to grannie inside my very next letter to her.

'I sit and watch a creature run through thickets endlessly.
It is the green grasshopper, making music – just for me.'

My mother had recently purchased a piano. But, like many another schoolboy, I preferred the natural music of the grasshopper's wings to the tinkling notes of a new piano.
E.F.H

Other books by Edward Forde Hickey

The Early Morning Light
A New Day Dawning
Footsteps in The Dew
A Bunch of Wild Roses
Tales from Tipperary
Reflections
From Time to Time
Old Faces

www.ingramcontent.com/pod-product-compliance
Lightning Source LLC
Chambersburg PA
CBHW042102060426

42446CB00046B/3466